Grandma's
BEST RECIPES

Publications International, Ltd.

Favorite Brand Name Recipes at www.fbnr.com

Microwave Cooking: Microwave ovens vary in wattage. Use the cooking times as guidelines and check for doneness before adding more time.

Preparation/Cooking Times: Preparation times are based on the approximate amount of time required to assemble the recipe before cooking, baking, chilling or serving. These times include preparation steps such as measuring, chopping and mixing. The fact that some preparations and cooking can be done simultaneously is taken into account. Preparation of optional ingredients and serving suggestions is not included.

CONTENTS

Great Country Breakfasts

Western Omelet

▌▌▌

½ cup finely chopped red or green bell pepper
⅓ cup cubed cooked potato
2 slices turkey bacon, diced
¼ teaspoon dried oregano leaves
2 teaspoons FLEISCHMANN'S® Original Margarine, divided
1 cup EGG BEATERS® Healthy Real Egg Substitute
Fresh oregano sprig, for garnish

In 8-inch nonstick skillet, over medium heat, sauté bell pepper, potato, turkey bacon and dried oregano in 1 teaspoon margarine until tender.* Remove from skillet; keep warm.

In same skillet, over medium heat, melt remaining margarine. Pour Egg Beaters® into skillet. Cook, lifting edges to allow uncooked portion to flow underneath. When almost set, spoon vegetable mixture over half of omelet. Fold other half over vegetable mixture; slide onto serving plate. Garnish with fresh oregano.

Makes 2 servings

*For frittata, sauté vegetables, turkey bacon and dried oregano in 2 teaspoons margarine. Pour Egg Beaters® evenly into skillet over vegetable mixture. Cook without stirring for 4 to 5 minutes or until cooked on bottom and almost set on top. Carefully turn frittata; cook for 1 to 2 minutes more or until done. Slide onto serving platter; cut into wedges to serve.

Prep Time: 15 minutes
Cook Time: 10 minutes

Western Omelet

Harvest Apple Oatmeal

Harvest Apple Oatmeal

■ ■ ■

- **1 cup apple juice**
- **1 cup water**
- **1 medium apple, cored, chopped**
- **1 cup uncooked old-fashioned oats**
- **¼ cup raisins**
- **⅛ teaspoon ground cinnamon**
- **⅛ teaspoon salt**

Microwave Directions

1. Combine apple juice, water and apple in 2-quart microwavable bowl. Microwave at HIGH 3 minutes, stirring halfway through cooking time.

2. Add oats, raisins, cinnamon and salt; stir until well blended.

3. Microwave at MEDIUM (50%) 4 to 5 minutes or until thick; stir before serving.

Makes 2 servings

Conventional Directions:
To prepare conventionally, bring apple juice, water and apple to a boil in medium saucepan over medium-high heat. Stir in oats, raisins, cinnamon and salt until well blended. Cook, uncovered, over medium heat 5 to 6 minutes or until thick, stirring occasionally.

Hearty Breakfast Custard Casserole

▮ ▮ ▮

1 pound (2 medium-large)
 Colorado baking potatoes
Salt and pepper
8 ounces low-fat bulk pork
 sausage, cooked and
 crumbled *or* 6 ounces
 finely diced lean ham *or*
 6 ounces turkey bacon,
 cooked and crumbled
⅓ cup julienne-sliced roasted
 red pepper *or* 1 jar
 (2 ounces) sliced
 pimientos, drained
3 eggs
1 cup low-fat milk
3 tablespoons chopped fresh
 chives or green onion
 tops *or* ¾ teaspoon dried
 thyme or oregano leaves
Salsa and low-fat sour
 cream or plain yogurt
 (optional)

Heat oven to 375°F. Grease 8- or 9-inch square baking dish or other small casserole. Peel potatoes and slice very thinly; arrange half of potatoes in baking dish. Sprinkle with salt and pepper. Cover with half of sausage. Arrange remaining potatoes on top; sprinkle with salt and pepper. Top with remaining sausage and red pepper. Beat eggs, milk and chives until blended. Pour over potatoes. Cover baking dish with foil and bake 35 to 45 minutes or until potatoes are tender. Uncover and bake 5 to 10 minutes more. Serve with salsa and sour cream, if desired.

Makes 4 to 5 servings

Favorite recipe from **Colorado Potato Administrative Committee**

Quiche Lorraine Florentine

▮ ▮ ▮

1 (10-ounce) package frozen
 chopped spinach, thawed
 and well drained
1 cup shredded Swiss cheese
 (4 ounces)
4 slices OSCAR MAYER®
 bacon, cooked and
 crumbled
2 tablespoons chopped green
 onions
1 (9-inch) unbaked pastry
 shell
3 eggs, slightly beaten
1 cup light cream or half-and-
 half
¼ cup GREY POUPON® Dijon
 Mustard

Combine spinach, cheese, bacon and green onions. Spoon mixture evenly into pastry shell.

In small bowl, blend eggs, cream and mustard. Pour evenly over spinach mixture. Bake at 375°F for 35 to 40 minutes or until knife inserted in center comes out clean. Let stand 10 minutes before serving. To serve, cut into wedges. *Makes 8 servings*

Apple & Raisin Oven Pancake

1 large baking apple, cored
  and thinly sliced
⅓ cup golden raisins
2 tablespoons packed brown
  sugar
½ teaspoon ground cinnamon
4 eggs
⅔ cup milk
⅔ cup all-purpose flour
2 tablespoons butter or
  margarine, melted
  Powdered sugar (optional)

Preheat oven to 350°F. Spray 9-inch pie plate with nonstick cooking spray.

Combine apple, raisins, brown sugar and cinnamon in medium bowl. Transfer to prepared pie plate.

Bake, uncovered, 10 to 15 minutes or until apple begins to soften. Remove from oven. *Increase oven temperature to 450°F.*

Meanwhile, whisk eggs, milk, flour and butter in medium bowl until blended. Pour batter over apple mixture.

Bake 15 minutes or until pancake is golden brown. Invert onto serving dish. Sprinkle with powdered sugar, if desired.   *Makes 6 servings*

Oven Breakfast Hash

2 pounds baking potatoes,
  unpeeled (5 or 6
  medium)
1 pound BOB EVANS® Original
  Recipe Roll Sausage
1 (12-ounce can) evaporated
  milk
⅓ cup chopped green onions
1 tablespoon Worcestershire
  sauce
½ teaspoon salt
¼ teaspoon black pepper
¼ cup dried bread crumbs
1 tablespoon melted butter or
  margarine
½ teaspoon paprika

Cook potatoes in boiling water until fork-tender. Drain and coarsely chop or mash. Preheat oven to 350°F. Crumble and cook sausage in medium skillet until browned. Drain and transfer to large bowl. Stir in potatoes, milk, green onions, Worcestershire sauce, salt and pepper. Pour into greased 2½- or 3-quart casserole dish. Sprinkle with bread crumbs; drizzle with melted butter. Sprinkle with paprika. Bake, uncovered, 30 to 35 minutes or until casserole bubbles and top is browned. Refrigerate leftovers.

Makes 6 to 8 servings

Apple & Raisin Oven Pancake

Stuffed French Toast with Apricot and Orange Marmalade Sauce

▊ ▊ ▊

Apricot and Orange
   Marmalade Sauce (recipe
   follows)
1 package (8 ounces) cream
   cheese, softened
½ cup (4 ounces) part-skim
   ricotta cheese
¼ cup orange marmalade
2 tablespoons sugar
1 loaf (16 ounces) Vienna
   bread
4 eggs
1 cup milk
1 teaspoon vanilla
   Grated nutmeg

1. Prepare Apricot and Orange Marmalade Sauce. Preheat oven to 475°F.

2. Beat cream cheese in medium bowl with electric mixer at medium speed until smooth. Beat in ricotta, marmalade and sugar.

3. Trim ends from bread; discard. Slice into 8 (1½-inch-thick) slices. Cut pocket in each slice by cutting through top crust and almost to bottom. Carefully fill each pocket with about 3 tablespoons cream cheese mixture.

4. Beat eggs in large shallow dish. Add milk and vanilla; whisk until blended. Dip 1 piece of bread at a time into egg mixture; turn over and allow to soak up egg mixture.

5. Place filled slices onto lightly greased baking sheet. Sprinkle with nutmeg. Bake 5 minutes or until golden on bottom. Turn slices over; sprinkle with nutmeg. Bake 3 to 5 minutes or until golden on bottom. Baked toast should feel just slightly crisp on surface. Serve with Apricot and Orange Marmalade Sauce.   *Makes 6 to 8 servings*

APRICOT AND ORANGE MARMALADE SAUCE

1 tablespoon butter
1½ cups chopped peeled fresh
   apricots or peaches
1 cup orange marmalade
½ teaspoon ground nutmeg

Melt butter in medium saucepan over medium-high heat. Add apricots; cook and stir 5 to 10 minutes or until fork-tender. Add marmalade and nutmeg; stir until marmalade is melted. Transfer mixture to food processor; process until apricots are finely chopped. Serve warm.

Makes about 2 cups

*Stuffed French Toast with Apricot
and Orange Marmalade Sauce*

Golden Apple French Toast

▌▌▌

1 Washington Golden
   Delicious apple, cored
   and sliced
½ cup apple juice
1 large egg, beaten
¼ teaspoon vanilla extract
2 slices bread
1 teaspoon cornstarch
⅛ teaspoon salt
⅛ teaspoon ground cardamom
1 tablespoon cold water

1. In small saucepan, combine apple slices and apple juice; heat to a simmer. Cook apple slices until tender but still retain their shape, about 8 minutes. Remove from heat and set aside while preparing French toast.

2. To make French toast, in wide shallow bowl, combine egg and vanilla. Dip bread slices in egg mixture to coat both sides. In nonstick skillet, cook bread slices until lightly browned on both sides. Remove French toast to serving plates; with slotted spoon, remove apple slices from apple juice and arrange on top of French toast; reserve apple juice in pan. To make syrup, combine cornstarch, salt, cardamom, and water; stir into reserved apple juice. Bring mixture to a boil, stirring constantly; cook until thickened and clear. Spoon syrup over apple slices and French toast and serve.

Makes 2 servings

Favorite recipe from **Washington Apple Commission**

Spinach and Cheese Brunch Squares

▌▌▌

1 box (11 ounces) pie crust
   mix
⅓ cup cold water
1 package (10 ounces) frozen
   chopped spinach, thawed
   and well drained
1⅓ cups *FRENCH'S®* French
   Fried Onions
1 cup (4 ounces) shredded
   Swiss cheese
1 container (8 ounces) low-
   fat sour cream
5 eggs
1 cup milk
1 tablespoon *FRENCH'S®*
   Zesty Deli Mustard
½ teaspoon salt
⅛ teaspoon ground black
   pepper

Preheat oven to 450°F. Line 13×9×2-inch baking pan with foil; spray with nonstick cooking spray. Combine pie crust mix and water in large bowl until moistened and crumbly. Using floured bottom of measuring cup, press mixture firmly into bottom of prepared pan. Prick with fork. Bake 20 minutes or until golden. *Reduce oven temperature to 350°F.*

Layer spinach, French Fried Onions and cheese over crust. Combine sour cream, eggs, milk, mustard, salt and pepper in medium bowl; mix until well blended. Pour over vegetable and cheese layers. Bake 30 minutes or until knife inserted in center comes out clean. Let stand 10 minutes. Cut into squares* to serve.

Makes 8 main-course servings

*To serve as appetizers, cut into 2-inch squares.

Prep Time: 20 minutes
Cook Time: 50 minutes
Stand Time: 10 minutes

Spinach and Cheese Brunch Square

KITCHEN TOOL TIME

What makes getting up in the morning easy? Fresh, steaming-hot homemade waffles—they're simple to make and so delicious too. In no time you can have a plate heaping with crispy waffles awaiting the topping of your choice. Waffles are perfect for breakfast, of course—but also try them for lunch, dinner and even dessert. Everyone loves butter and syrup toppings, but how about adding your favorite fresh fruit to your morning waffles. Top those lunch or dinner waffles with anything you like—tuna salad—to make a quick and hearty meal. And who can resist ice cream and chocolate syrup on top of waffles for a grand finale.

Waffle makers come in different sizes and shapes but all work just about the same. The magic of the waffle maker is that it takes a basic batter and turns it into a crispy and puffy treat perfect for everyone's tastes. Let your family and friends complement your creation with their favorite toppings. Follow the helpful tips below to make perfect waffles in a snap.

• Before you begin cooking, always coat the inside of the waffle maker (grid plate) with nonstick cooking spray or wipe with a paper towel lightly coated with oil. Be careful that you don't get a buildup of oil on the grid plate as this will impart an off flavor to your waffles.

• Once the waffle maker is hot, it's time to add the batter. When doing so, do not fill the entire grid plate with batter as there will be no room for expansion and batter will overflow the sides of the waffle maker.

• Every waffle maker has a signal to let you know when the waffle is done. As a general rule, however, a waffle is done when steam no longer escapes from the waffle maker and the waffle is lightly browned and crispy.

• Don't throw away leftover waffles—simply save them for a quick breakfast, dinner or dessert. Let them cool completely and then wrap in plastic wrap and freeze. To serve them, pop the frozen waffles into the toaster.

• Finally, be sure that the waffle maker is clean before storing it. For simple and quick cleanup, unplug the waffle maker while it is still warm. Slightly dampen several paper towels and place them on the grill plate and close the waffle maker. Once the steam stops, open the waffle maker and remove the paper towels—your waffle maker is sparkling clean in just seconds.

Roman Meal® Waffles

▌▌▌

1⅓ cups all-purpose flour
2 tablespoons sugar
1 tablespoon baking powder
½ teaspoon salt
⅔ cup ROMAN MEAL® Cereal
1½ cups milk (may be skim milk)
⅓ cup vegetable oil
2 stiffly beaten egg whites

Preheat waffle iron. In medium bowl, combine flour, sugar, baking powder, salt and cereal. Mix together milk and oil; add all at once to dry ingredients. Mix well. Fold in egg whites. Pour batter onto hot waffle iron. *Makes 8 to 10 waffles, 4½ inches each*

Waffle

Waffles with Stawberry Sauce

▌▌▌

2¼ cups all-purpose flour
2 tablespoons sugar
1 tablespoon baking powder
½ teaspoon salt
2 eggs, beaten
¼ cup vegetable oil
2 cups milk
Strawberry Sauce (recipe follows)

1. Preheat waffle iron; grease lightly.

2. Sift flour, sugar, baking powder and salt into large bowl. Combine eggs, oil and milk in medium bowl. Stir liquid ingredients into dry ingredients until moistened.

3. For each waffle, pour about ¾ cup of batter into waffle iron. Close lid and bake until steaming stops.* Serve with Strawberry Sauce.
Makes about 6 round waffles

*Check the manufacturer's directions for recommended amount of batter and baking time.

STRAWBERRY SAUCE
1 pint strawberries, hulled
2 to 3 tablespoons sugar
1 tablespoon strawberry- or orange-flavored liqueur (optional)

Combine strawberries, sugar and liqueur in blender or food processor. Cover; process until strawberries are puréed.
Makes 1½ cups

Chocolate Waffles

■ ■ ■

2 cups all-purpose flour
¼ cup unsweetened cocoa
powder
2 tablespoons sugar
1 tablespoon baking powder
½ teaspoon salt
2 cups milk
2 eggs, beaten
¼ cup vegetable oil
1 teaspoon vanilla extract
Raspberry Syrup (recipe
follows)

1. Preheat waffle iron; grease lightly.

2. Sift flour, cocoa, sugar, baking powder and salt into large bowl. Combine milk, eggs, oil and vanilla in small bowl. Stir liquid ingredients into dry ingredients until moistened.

3. For each waffle, pour about ¾ cup batter into waffle iron. Close lid and bake until steaming stops.* Serve with Raspberry Syrup.

Makes about 6 waffles

Check manufacturer's directions for recommended amount of batter and baking time.

RASPBERRY SYRUP
1 cup water
1 cup sugar
1 package (10 ounces) frozen
raspberries in syrup

1. Combine water and sugar in large saucepan. Cook over medium heat, stirring constantly, until sugar has dissolved. Continue cooking until mixture thickens slightly, about 10 minutes.

2. Stir in frozen raspberries; cook, stirring, until berries are thawed. Bring to a boil; continue cooking until syrup thickens slightly, about 5 to 10 minutes. Serve warm.

Makes about 1⅓ cups

Country Recipe Biscuits

■ ■ ■

2 cups all-purpose flour
1 tablespoon baking powder
½ cup prepared HIDDEN
VALLEY® Original Ranch®
salad dressing
½ cup buttermilk

Preheat oven to 425°F. In small bowl, sift together flour and baking powder. Make a well in flour mixture; add salad dressing and buttermilk. Stir with fork until dough forms a ball. Drop by rounded spoonfuls onto ungreased baking sheet. Bake until lightly browned, 12 to 15 minutes.

Makes 12 biscuits

Apple Ring Coffee Cake

■ ■ ■

3 cups all-purpose flour
1 teaspoon baking soda
1 teaspoon salt
1 teaspoon ground cinnamon
1 cup walnuts, chopped
1½ cups granulated sugar
1 cup vegetable oil
2 teaspoons vanilla
2 eggs
2 medium tart apples, peeled, cored and chopped
Powdered sugar for garnish

Preheat oven to 325°F. Grease 10-inch tube pan; set aside.

Sift flour, baking soda, salt and cinnamon into large bowl. Stir in walnuts; set aside.

Combine granulated sugar, oil, vanilla and eggs in medium bowl. Stir in apples. Stir into flour mixture just until moistened.

Spoon batter into prepared pan, spreading evenly. Bake 1 hour or until toothpick inserted in center comes out clean. Cool cake in pan on wire rack 10 minutes. Loosen edges with metal spatula, if necessary. Remove from pan; cool completely on rack.

Transfer to serving plate. Sprinkle with powdered sugar and serve immediately. Store leftover cake in airtight container.

Makes 12 servings

Lemon Poppy Seed Muffins

■ ■ ■

2½ cups all-purpose flour
½ cup sugar
2 tablespoons poppy seed
1 tablespoon baking powder
1¼ cups skim milk
¼ cup FLEISCHMANN'S® Original Margarine, melted
¼ cup EGG BEATERS® Healthy Real Egg Substitute
1 tablespoon grated lemon peel

In large bowl, combine flour, sugar, poppy seed and baking powder; set aside.

In small bowl, combine milk, margarine, Egg Beaters and lemon peel. Stir into flour mixture just until moistened. Spoon batter into 12 lightly greased 2½-inch muffin pan cups.* Bake at 400°F for 20 to 22 minutes or until lightly browned. Serve warm.

Makes 1 dozen muffins

For miniature muffins, use 36 (1½-inch) muffin-pan cups. Reduce baking time to 14 to 16 minutes.

Prep Time: 15 minutes
Cook Time: 22 minutes

Sour Cream Coffee Cake with Brandy-Soaked Cherries

■ ■ ■

Streusel Topping (recipe
    follows)
3¼ cups all-purpose flour,
    divided
  1 cup dry sweet or sour
    cherries
½ cup brandy
1½ cups sugar
  ¾ cup butter or margarine
  3 eggs
  1 container (16 ounces) sour
    cream
  1 tablespoon vanilla
  2 teaspoons baking powder
  2 teaspoons baking soda
  ¼ teaspoon salt

1. Prepare Streusel Topping; set aside.

2. Preheat oven to 350°F. Grease 10-inch tube pan with removable bottom. Sprinkle ¼ cup flour into pan, rotating pan to evenly coat bottom and sides of pan. Discard any remaining flour.

3. Bring cherries and brandy to a boil in small saucepan. Cover; remove from heat. Let stand 20 to 30 minutes or until cherries are tender. Drain; discard any remaining brandy.

4. Beat sugar and butter in large bowl with electric mixer at medium speed until light and fluffy. Add eggs, 1 at a time, beating until thoroughly incorporated. Beat in sour cream and vanilla. Add remaining 3 cups flour, baking powder, baking soda and salt. Beat with electric mixer at low speed until just blended. Stir in cherries.

5. Spoon ½ of batter into prepared tube pan. Sprinkle with ½ of Streusel Topping. Repeat with remaining batter and Streusel Topping. Bake 1 hour or until toothpick inserted into center comes out clean.

6. Cool in pan on wire rack 10 minutes. Remove from pan. Serve warm or at room temperature. Garnish as desired.   *Makes 16 servings*

STREUSEL TOPPING
  1 cup chopped walnuts or
    pecans
  ½ cup packed brown sugar
  1 teaspoon ground cinnamon
  ½ teaspoon ground nutmeg
  2 tablespoons melted butter
    or margarine

Combine nuts, brown sugar, cinnamon and nutmeg in small bowl. Drizzle mixture with butter and toss with fork until evenly mixed.

Sour Cream Coffee Cake with Brandy-Soaked Cherries

Apple and Walnut Spiced Muffins

▌▌▌

1 cup raisins
2 cups all-purpose flour
1 cup oatmeal
⅔ cup sugar
2½ teaspoons baking powder
½ teaspoon salt
½ teaspoon ground cinnamon
½ teaspoon ground allspice
¼ teaspoon ground nutmeg
4 to 5 small apples
1 egg
2 egg whites
¼ cup canola oil or vegetable oil
½ cup chopped California walnuts

Preheat oven to 350°F. Grease muffin tins or spray with nonstick cooking spray.

Pour hot water over raisins in a small bowl and let sit 10 minutes; drain well and set aside.

Meanwhile, in medium bowl, combine flour, oatmeal, sugar, baking powder, salt, cinnamon, allspice and nutmeg. Stir and toss to combine; set aside.

Peel and core apples. Grate coarsely—you need about 2 generous cups, lightly pressed down. Combine grated apples, egg, egg whites, oil, walnuts and raisins; beat to blend. Add to combined dry ingredients and raisins; stir just until blended and moistened—the batter will be very stiff. Spoon into prepared muffin tins, filling about three-quarters full. Bake 20 to 25 minutes, or until wooden pick inserted in muffin comes out clean. Cool 5 minutes in pan; remove and serve warm.

Makes 12 muffins

Favorite recipe from **Walnut Marketing Board**

Banana Nut Bread

▌▌▌

2 extra-ripe, large DOLE® Bananas, peeled
⅓ cup butter
⅔ cup sugar
2 eggs
2 cups all-purpose flour
2 teaspoons baking powder
½ teaspoon baking soda
½ cup buttermilk
¾ cup chopped nuts

• Purée bananas in blender (1¼ cups). Cream butter and sugar until light and fluffy. Beat in bananas and eggs. Combine flour, baking powder and baking soda. Add dry ingredients to banana mixture alternately in thirds with buttermilk, blending well after each addition. Stir in nuts.

• Pour into greased 9×5-inch loaf pan. Bake in 350°F oven 50 to 60 minutes or until wooden toothpick inserted in center comes out clean. Cool in pan on wire rack 10 minutes. Remove from pan and cool completely. *Makes 1 loaf*

Orange-Currant Scones

███

1½ cups all-purpose flour
¼ cup plus 1 teaspoon sugar,
   divided
1 teaspoon baking powder
¼ teaspoon salt
¼ teaspoon baking soda
⅓ cup currants
1 tablespoon grated fresh
   orange peel
6 tablespoons chilled butter
   or margarine, cut into
   small pieces
½ cup buttermilk, plain
   yogurt, or regular or
   nonfat sour cream

1. Preheat oven to 425°F. Combine flour, ¼ cup sugar, baking powder, salt and baking soda in large bowl. Stir in currants and orange peel.

2. Cut in butter with pastry blender or 2 knives until mixture resembles coarse crumbs. Stir in buttermilk. Stir until mixture forms soft dough that clings together. (Dough will be tacky.)

3. Lightly flour hands and shape dough into a ball. Pat dough into 8-inch round on lightly greased baking sheet. Cut dough into 8 wedges with floured chef's knife.

4. Sprinkle wedges with remaining 1 teaspoon sugar. Bake 18 to 20 minutes or until lightly browned.

Makes 8 scones

Orange-Currant Scone

Vegetable Soup with Delicious Dumplings

SOUP
- 2 tablespoons WESSON® Vegetable Oil
- 1 cup diced onion
- ¾ cup sliced celery
- 7 cups homemade chicken broth *or* 4 (14½-ounce) cans chicken broth
- 2 (14.5-ounce) cans HUNT'S® Stewed Tomatoes
- ½ teaspoon garlic powder
- ½ teaspoon salt
- ½ teaspoon fines herbs seasoning
- ⅛ teaspoon pepper
- 1 (16-ounce) bag frozen mixed vegetables
- 1 (15½-ounce) can HUNT'S® Red Kidney Beans, drained
- ⅓ cup uncooked long-grain rice

DUMPLINGS
- 2 cups all-purpose flour
- 3 tablespoons baking powder
- 1 teaspoon salt
- ⅔ cup milk
- ⅓ cup WESSON® Vegetable Oil
- 1½ teaspoons chopped fresh parsley

Soup
In a large Dutch oven, heat Wesson® Oil. Add onion and celery; sauté until crisp-tender. Stir in *next 6* ingredients, ending with pepper; bring to a boil. Add vegetables, beans and rice. Reduce heat; cover and simmer 15 to 20 minutes or until rice is cooked and vegetables are tender.

Dumplings
Meanwhile, in a medium bowl, combine flour, baking powder and salt; blend well. Add milk, Wesson® Oil and parsley; mix until batter forms a ball in the bowl. Drop dough by rounded tablespoons into simmering soup. Cook, covered, 10 minutes; remove lid and cook an additional 10 minutes.
Makes 10 servings

Vegetable Soup with Delicious Dumplings

Pork and Vegetable Stew with Noodles

Pork and Vegetable Stew with Noodles

▌▌▌

1 pound lean boneless pork
2 tablespoons vegetable oil
3 cups beef broth
3 tablespoons chopped fresh parsley, divided
1 can (14½ ounces) stewed tomatoes
1 large carrot, sliced
3 green onions, sliced
2 teaspoons Dijon mustard
¼ teaspoon rubbed sage
⅛ teaspoon black pepper
3 cups uncooked noodles
1 teaspoon butter or margarine
2 tablespoons all-purpose flour
⅓ cup cold water
Apples and parsley for garnish

Cut pork into ¾-inch cubes. Heat oil in large saucepan over medium-high heat. Add meat; brown, stirring frequently. Add beef broth. Stir in 1 tablespoon chopped parsley, tomatoes, carrot, onions, mustard, sage and pepper. Bring to a boil over high heat. Reduce heat to medium-low; simmer, uncovered, 30 minutes.

Meanwhile, cook noodles according to package directions; drain. Add reserved 2 tablespoons chopped parsley and butter; toss lightly. Keep warm until ready to serve.

Stir flour into cold water in cup until smooth. Stir into stew. Cook and stir over medium heat until slightly thickened. To serve, spoon noodles onto each plate. Ladle stew over noodles.

Makes 4 servings

Country Bean Soup

▌▌▌

1¼ cups dried navy beans or lima beans, rinsed and drained
4 ounces salt pork or fully cooked ham, chopped
¼ cup chopped onion
½ teaspoon dried oregano leaves
¼ teaspoon salt
¼ teaspoon ground ginger
¼ teaspoon dried sage
¼ teaspoon ground black pepper
2 cups fat-free (skim) milk
2 tablespoons butter

1. Place navy beans in large saucepan; add enough water to cover beans. Bring to a boil; reduce heat and simmer 2 minutes. Remove from heat; cover and let stand for 1 hour. (Or, cover beans with water and soak overnight.)

2. Drain beans and return to saucepan. Stir in 2½ cups water, salt pork, onion, oregano, salt, ginger, sage and pepper. Bring to a boil; reduce heat. Cover and simmer 2 to 2½ hours or until beans are tender. (If necessary, add more water during cooking.) Add milk and butter, stirring until mixture is heated through and butter is melted. Season with additional salt and pepper, if desired. *Makes 6 servings*

Shaker Chicken and Noodle Soup

▌▌▌

13 cups chicken broth, divided
¼ cup dry vermouth
¼ cup butter or margarine
1 cup heavy cream
1 package (12 ounces) egg noodles
1 cup thinly sliced celery
1½ cups water
¾ cup all-purpose flour
2 cups diced cooked chicken
Salt and black pepper
¼ cup finely chopped parsley (optional)

1. Combine 1 cup broth, vermouth and butter in small saucepan. Bring to a boil over high heat. Continue to boil 15 to 20 minutes or until liquid is reduced to ¼ cup and has a syrupy consistency. Stir in cream. Set aside.

2. Bring remaining 12 cups broth to a boil in Dutch oven. Add noodles and celery; cook until noodles are just tender.

3. Combine water and flour in medium bowl until smooth. Stir into broth mixture. Boil 2 minutes, stirring constantly.

4. Stir in reserved cream mixture; add chicken. Season with salt and pepper. Heat just to serving temperature. Do not boil. Sprinkle with parsley, if desired. Garnish as desired. *Makes 15 servings*

Cream of Chicken and Wild Rice Soup

▮ ▮ ▮

½ cup uncooked wild rice
 5 cups canned chicken broth, divided
¼ cup butter
 1 large carrot, sliced
 1 medium onion, chopped
 2 ribs celery, chopped
¼ pound fresh mushrooms, sliced
 2 tablespoons all-purpose flour
¼ teaspoon salt
¼ teaspoon white pepper
1½ cups chopped cooked chicken
¼ cup dry sherry

1. Rinse rice thoroughly in fine strainer under cold running water; drain.

2. Combine 2½ cups chicken broth and rice in 2-quart saucepan. Bring to a boil over medium-high heat. Reduce heat to low; simmer, covered, 1 hour or until rice is tender. Drain; set aside.

3. Melt butter in 3-quart saucepan over medium heat. Add carrot; cook and stir 3 minutes. Add onion, celery and mushrooms; cook and stir 3 to 4 minutes until vegetables are tender. Remove from heat. Whisk in flour, salt and pepper until smooth.

4. Gradually stir in remaining 2½ cups chicken broth. Bring to a boil over medium heat; cook and stir 1 minute or until thickened. Stir in chicken and sherry. Reduce heat to low; simmer, uncovered, 3 minutes or until heated through.

5. Spoon ¼ cup cooked rice into each serving bowl. Ladle soup over rice.

Makes 4 to 6 servings

Serve It With Style!

*F*or a hearty winter meal, serve this soup in a hollowed-out toasted French roll or small round sourdough loaves.

Cream of Chicken and Wild Rice Soup

Bistro Stew

■ ■ ■

1 pound boneless beef sirloin,
    cut into 1½-inch pieces
3 tablespoons all-purpose
    flour
6 slices bacon, cut into
    1-inch pieces (about
    ¼ pound)
2 cloves garlic, crushed
3 carrots, peeled and cut into
    1-inch pieces (about
    1½ cups)
2 tablespoons Dijon Mustard
1¼ cup beef broth or lower
    sodium beef broth
12 small mushrooms
1½ cups green onions, cut into
    1½-inch pieces
    Breadsticks, optional

1. Coat beef with flour, shaking off excess; set aside.

2. In large skillet, over medium heat, cook bacon just until done; pour off excess fat. Add beef and garlic; cook until browned. Add carrots, mustard and beef broth. Heat to a boil; reduce heat. Cover; simmer 30 minutes or until carrots are tender, stirring occasionally. Stir in mushrooms and green onions; cook 10 minutes more, stirring occasionally. Serve with breadsticks, if desired.

Makes 4 servings

Split Pea Soup

■ ■ ■

1 package (16 ounces) dried
    green or yellow split peas
1 pound smoked pork hocks
    or 4 ounces smoked
    sausage link, sliced and
    quartered *or* 1 meaty
    ham bone
7 cups water
1 medium onion, chopped
2 medium carrots, chopped
¾ teaspoon salt
½ teaspoon dried basil leaves
¼ teaspoon dried oregano
    leaves
¼ teaspoon black pepper
    Ham and carrot strips for
    garnish

Rinse peas thoroughly in colander under cold running water, picking out any debris or blemished peas. Place peas, pork hocks and water in 5-quart Dutch oven.

Add onion, carrots, salt, basil, oregano and pepper to Dutch oven. Bring to a boil over high heat. Reduce heat to medium-low; simmer, uncovered, 1 hour 15 minutes or until peas are tender, stirring occasionally. Stir frequently near end of cooking to keep soup from scorching.

Remove pork hocks; cool. Cut meat into bite-size pieces.

Carefully ladle 3 cups hot soup into food processor or blender; cover and process until mixture is smooth.

Return puréed soup and meat to Dutch oven. (If soup is too thick, add a little water until desired consistency is reached.) Heat through. Ladle into bowls. Garnish, if desired.

Makes 6 servings

Golden Potato Chowder

█ █ █

6 cups cubed peeled
   potatoes
5 tablespoons butter or
   margarine
2 tablespoons all-purpose
   flour
1 cup chopped onion
1 cup chopped carrots
1 cup chopped celery
1 cup sliced mushrooms
4 cups chicken broth
1 teaspoon salt
½ teaspoon dried marjoram
   leaves
½ teaspoon hot pepper sauce
   White pepper to taste
1 pound BOB EVANS® Original
   Recipe Roll Sausage
   Croutons for garnish
   (optional)

Place potatoes in large saucepan with water to cover. Bring to a boil over high heat; boil about 8 minutes or until potatoes are fork-tender. Drain and return to saucepan. Stir in butter and flour over medium heat. Add onion, carrots, celery and mushrooms; cook about 10 minutes or until potatoes begin to brown, stirring frequently. Stir in broth, salt, marjoram, hot pepper sauce and white pepper; simmer 30 minutes. Meanwhile, crumble and cook sausage in medium skillet until browned. Drain off any drippings. Blend or crush vegetables with potato masher in saucepan just until chunky. Stir sausage into soup. Serve hot with croutons, if desired. Refrigerate leftovers.

Makes 8 servings

Cook's Nook

Leftover soup can be a quick and healthy lunch when your're on the go. Place 1 cup of soup in a 2-cup microwavable cup or bowl. Heat at HIGH 1 to 1½ minutes; stir.

Black and White Chili

▊ ▊ ▊

Nonstick cooking spray
1 pound chicken tenders, cut
    into ¾-inch pieces
1 cup coarsely chopped onion
1 can (15½ ounces) Great
    Northern beans, drained
1 can (15 ounces) black
    beans, drained
1 can (14½ ounces) Mexican-
    style stewed tomatoes,
    undrained
2 tablespoons Texas-style
    chili powder seasoning
    mix

1. Spray large saucepan with cooking spray; heat over medium heat until hot. Add chicken and onion; cook and stir over medium to medium-high heat 5 to 8 minutes or until chicken is browned and no longer pink in center.

2. Stir remaining ingredients into saucepan; bring to a boil. Reduce heat to low; simmer, uncovered, 10 minutes.
Makes 6 (1-cup) servings

Serving Suggestion: For a change of pace, this delicious chili is excellent served over cooked rice or pasta.

Cook's Notes

This delicious chili only takes 30 minutes to prepare. It is a great quick weeknight meal!

Black and White Chili

YEAST Rise the on BREADS

Garlic and Herb Parmesan Buns

8 BUNS INGREDIENTS
1¼ cups water
  1 tablespoon sugar
1½ teaspoons salt
  1 teaspoon garlic powder
  2 teaspoons Italian herbs
  ⅓ cup grated Parmesan
    cheese
  3 cups bread flour
  1 tablespoon rapid-rise yeast

12 BUNS INGREDIENTS
1½ cups water
  2 tablespoons sugar
  2 teaspoons salt
1½ teaspoons garlic powder
  1 tablespoon Italian herbs
  ½ cup grated Parmesan
    cheese
  4 cups bread flour
  1 tablespoon rapid-rise yeast

TOPPING
  1 to 2 tablespoons grated
    Parmesan cheese

1. Measure carefully, placing all ingredients except topping in bread machine pan in order specified by owner's manual. Program dough cycle setting; press start.

2. Turn out dough onto lightly oiled surface. Cut dough into 8 pieces for small batch or 12 pieces for large batch. Shape into smooth balls. Place on greased baking sheet; flatten slightly. Let rise in warm place 45 minutes or until doubled.

3. Preheat oven to 400°F. Brush buns with water; sprinkle tops with pinch of cheese. Bake 15 minutes or until lightly browned. Serve warm or transfer onto wire rack to cool completely.

Makes 8 or 12 buns

Garlic and Herb Parmesan Buns

Honey Wheat Brown-and-Serve Rolls

▌▌▌

2 packages active dry yeast
1 teaspoon sugar
¾ cup warm water (105° to 115°F)
2 cups whole wheat flour
2 to 3 cups all-purpose flour, divided
¼ cup vegetable shortening
¼ cup honey
1 teaspoon salt
1 egg

Sprinkle yeast and sugar over warm water in small bowl; stir until yeast is dissolved. Let stand 5 minutes until mixture is bubbly. Combine whole wheat flour and 2 cups all-purpose flour in medium bowl. Measure 1½ cups flour mixture into large bowl. Add yeast mixture, shortening, honey, salt and egg. Beat with electric mixer at low speed until smooth. Increase mixer speed to medium; beat 2 minutes, scraping down side of bowl once. Reduce speed to low; beat in 1 cup flour mixture. Increase mixer speed to medium; beat 2 minutes, scraping down side of bowl once. Stir in remaining flour mixture and enough additional all-purpose flour (about ¼ cup) with wooden spoon to make a soft dough.

Turn dough out onto lightly floured surface. Knead 8 to 10 minutes or until smooth and elastic, adding more flour to prevent sticking, if necessary. Shape dough into a ball; place in large greased bowl. Turn once to grease surface. Cover with clean kitchen towel. Let rise in warm place (80° to 85°F) about 1½ hours or until doubled in bulk. Punch down dough. Turn dough onto lightly floured surface. Knead dough several turns to remove all the large air bubbles; cover and let rest 15 minutes. Meanwhile, grease 24 muffin cups.

Divide dough into 24 pieces. Cut 1 piece into thirds. Roll each third into a ball. Place 3 balls in each muffin cup. Repeat with remaining dough. Cover and let rise in warm place about 30 minutes until doubled in bulk.

Preheat oven to 275°F.* Bake 20 to 25 minutes or until rolls are set but not brown. Immediately remove rolls from muffin cups and cool completely on wire racks. Store in resealable plastic food storage bags in refrigerator or freezer.

To bake rolls, thaw rolls if frozen. Preheat oven to 400°F. Grease large jelly-roll pan. Place rolls on jelly-roll pan. Bake 8 to 10 minutes or until golden brown. *Makes 24 rolls*

*To bake rolls immediately, preheat oven to 375°F. Bake 15 to 20 minutes or until golden brown. Immediately remove from pan. Serve warm.

Whole Wheat Loaves

■ ■ ■

3 cups whole wheat flour,
    divided
2¼ to 2¾ cups all-purpose
    flour, divided
½ cup wheat germ
2 packages active dry yeast
2 teaspoons salt
1¼ cups milk
1 cup water
⅓ cup honey
¼ cup butter or margarine

1. Combine 2 cups whole wheat flour, 1 cup all-purpose flour, wheat germ, yeast and salt in large bowl; set aside.

2. Combine milk, water, honey and butter in 2-quart saucepan. Heat over low heat until mixture is 120° to 130°F. (Butter does not need to completely melt.)

3. Gradually beat milk mixture into flour mixture with electric mixer at medium speed. Reduce speed to low. Beat in remaining 1 cup whole wheat flour. Beat 2 minutes at medium speed.

4. Stir in enough additional all-purpose flour, about 1¼ cups, to make soft dough.

5. Turn out dough onto lightly floured surface; flatten slightly. Knead dough 8 to 10 minutes or until smooth and elastic, adding remaining ½ cup all-purpose flour to prevent sticking if necessary.

6. Shape dough into a ball; place in large greased bowl. Turn dough over so that top is greased. Cover with towel; let rise in warm place about 1 hour or until doubled in bulk.

7. Punch down dough. Knead dough on lightly floured surface 1 minute. Cut dough into halves. Cover with towel; let rest 10 minutes. Grease 2 (8½×4½-inch) loaf pans; set aside.

8. Roll out one half of dough into 38×12-inch rectangle with lightly floured rolling pin. Starting with 1 (8-inch) side, roll up dough jelly-roll style. Pinch seam and ends to seal. Place loaf, seam side down, in prepared pan, tucking ends under. Repeat with remaining dough. Cover with towel; let rise in warm place about 45 minutes or until doubled in bulk.

9. Preheat oven to 350°F. Bake 30 to 35 minutes or until loaves are browned and sound hollow when tapped. Immediately remove from pans; cool completely on wire racks.

Makes 2 loaves

Sesame-Onion Twists

▌▌▌

2 tablespoons butter or
    margarine
1½ cups finely chopped onions
  ¼ teaspoon paprika
  1 loaf (16 ounces) frozen
    bread dough, thawed
  1 egg, beaten
  1 tablespoon sesame seeds

1. Grease large baking sheet; set aside. Melt butter in medium skillet over medium heat until foamy. Add onions and paprika; cook until onions are tender, stirring occasionally. Remove from heat.

2. Spray work surface with nonstick cooking spray. Roll thawed bread dough into 14×12-inch rectangle.

3. Spread onion mixture on one side of dough. Fold dough over onion mixture to make 14×6-inch rectangle.

4. Pinch 14-inch side of dough to seal. Cut dough into 14 lengthwise strips.

5. Gently twist dough strip two times and place on prepared sheet. Press both ends of strip down on cookie sheet. Repeat with remaining strips.

6. Cover with towel. Let twists rise in warm place about 40 minutes or until doubled in bulk. Brush with egg; sprinkle with sesame seeds.

7. Preheat oven to 375°F. Bake 15 to 18 minutes or until golden brown. Serve immediately.

Makes 14 twists

For a change of pace, shape the dough strips into circles, hearts or whatever you desire.

Sesame-Onion Twists

Many Grains Bread

▮▮▮

2¾ to 3¼ cups all-purpose
    flour, divided
3 cups graham flour, divided
2 packages RED STAR®
    Active Dry Yeast or
    QUICK•RISE™ Yeast
4 teaspoons salt
3 cups water
½ cup dark molasses
¼ cup vegetable oil
½ cup buckwheat flour
½ cup rye flour
½ cup soy flour
½ cup yellow cornmeal
½ cup quick rolled oats
    Butter

Combine 1½ cups all-purpose flour and 2 cups graham flour, yeast and salt in large bowl; mix well. Heat water, molasses and oil in large saucepan over medium heat until very warm (120° to 130°F). Add to flour mixture. Blend at low speed until moistened; beat 3 minutes at medium speed. By hand, gradually stir in buckwheat, rye and soy flours, cornmeal, oats, remaining graham flour and enough remaining all-purpose flour to make a firm dough. Knead on floured surface 5 to 8 minutes. Place in large greased bowl, turning to grease top. Cover with clean kitchen towel; let rise in warm place about 1 hour or until double in bulk (about 30 minutes for QUICK•RISE™ Yeast).

Punch down dough. Divide into 2 parts. On lightly floured surface, shape each half into round loaf.

Place loaves on large greased baking sheet. Cover; let rise in warm place about 30 minutes or until double in bulk (15 minutes for QUICK•RISE™ Yeast).

Preheat oven to 375°F. With sharp knife, make cross slash across top of each loaf. Bake 35 to 40 minutes until bread sounds hollow when tapped. If bread starts to become too dark, cover loosely with foil during last 5 to 10 minutes of baking. Remove from baking sheet. Brush with butter; cool on wire racks.

Makes 2 round loaves

Savory Cheese Bread

███

6 to 7 cups flour, divided
2 tablespoons sugar
4 teaspoons instant minced onion
2 teaspoons salt
2 packages active dry yeast
½ teaspoon caraway seeds
1¾ cups milk
½ cup water
3 tablespoons butter or margarine
1 teaspoon TABASCO® brand Pepper Sauce
2 cups (8 ounces) shredded sharp Cheddar cheese, divided
1 egg, lightly beaten

In large bowl of electric mixer combine 2½ cups flour, sugar, onion, salt, yeast and caraway seeds. In small saucepan combine milk, water and butter. Heat milk mixture until very warm (120° to 130°F.); stir in TABASCO® Sauce.

With mixer at medium speed gradually add milk mixture to dry ingredients; beat 2 minutes. Add 1 cup flour. Beat at high speed 2 minutes. With wooden spoon stir in 1½ cups cheese and enough flour to make a stiff dough. Turn dough out onto lightly floured surface. Knead 8 to 10 minutes or until dough is smooth and elastic, adding as much remaining flour as needed to prevent sticking. Place dough in large greased bowl and turn once to grease surface. Cover with towel; let rise in warm place (90° to 100°F.) 1 hour or until doubled in bulk.

Punch dough down. Divide dough into 16 equal pieces; shape each piece into a ball. Place half the balls in well-greased 10-inch tube pan. Sprinkle with remaining ½ cup cheese. Arrange remaining balls on top. Cover with towel; let rise in warm place 45 minutes or until doubled in bulk. Preheat oven to 375°F. Brush dough with egg. Bake 40 to 50 minutes or until golden brown. Remove from pan. Cool completely on wire rack.

Makes 1 (10-inch) round loaf

Take Comfort in Casseroles

Shepherd's Pie

∎ ∎ ∎

1⅓ cups instant mashed potato
     buds
1⅔ cups milk
  2 tablespoons margarine or
     butter
  1 teaspoon salt, divided
  1 pound ground beef
  ¼ teaspoon black pepper
  1 jar (12 ounces) beef gravy
  1 package (10 ounces) frozen
     mixed vegetables,
     thawed and drained
  ¾ cup grated Parmesan
     cheese

1. Preheat broiler. Prepare
4 servings of mashed potatoes
according to package directions
using milk, margarine and
½ teaspoon salt.

2. While mashed potatoes are
cooking, brown meat in
medium broilerproof skillet
over medium-high heat,
stirring to separate meat. Drain
drippings. Sprinkle meat with
remaining ½ teaspoon salt and
pepper. Add gravy and
vegetables; mix well. Cook over
medium-low heat 5 minutes or
until hot.

3. Spoon prepared potatoes
around outside edge of skillet,
leaving 3-inch circle in center.
Sprinkle cheese evenly over
potatoes. Broil 4 to 5 inches
from heat source 3 minutes or
until cheese is golden brown
and meat mixture is bubbly.
Makes 4 servings

Prep & Cook Time: 28 minutes

Shepherd's Pie

Pork Chops and Apple Stuffing Bake

■ ■ ■

6 (¾-inch-thick) boneless
pork loin chops (about
1½ pounds)
¼ teaspoon salt
⅛ teaspoon black pepper
1 tablespoon vegetable oil
1 small onion, chopped
2 ribs celery, chopped
2 Granny Smith apples,
peeled, cored and
coarsely chopped (about
2 cups)
1 can (14½ ounces) reduced-
sodium chicken broth
1 can (10¾ ounces)
condensed cream of
celery soup, undiluted
¼ cup dry white wine
6 cups herb-seasoned stuffing
cubes

Preheat oven to 375°F. Spray
13×9-inch baking dish with
nonstick cooking spray.

Season both sides of pork
chops with salt and pepper.
Heat oil in large deep skillet
over medium-high heat until
hot. Add chops and cook until
browned on both sides, turning
once. Remove chops from
skillet; set aside.

Add onion and celery to same
skillet. Cook and stir 3 minutes
or until onion is tender. Add
apples; cook and stir 1 minute.
Add broth, soup and wine; mix
well. Bring to a simmer; remove
from heat. Stir in stuffing cubes
until evenly moistened.

Pour stuffing mixture into
prepared dish, spreading
evenly. Place pork chops on top
of stuffing; pour any
accumulated juices over chops.

Cover tightly with foil and bake
30 to 40 minutes or until pork
chops are juicy and barely pink
in center.   *Makes 6 servings*

Pork Chop and Stuffing Bake

Chicken Bourguignonne

Tamale Beef Pie

■ ■ ■

1½ pounds ground beef
1 package (1¼ ounces) taco seasoning mix
1 can (11 ounces) whole kernel corn, drained
1 can (10 ounces) tomatoes and green chilies
1 cup chopped green or red bell peppers
2⅔ cups FRENCH'S® French Fried Onions, divided
1 package (8½ ounces) corn muffin mix
½ cup (2 ounces) shredded Cheddar cheese

Preheat oven to 400°F. Brown ground beef in large nonstick skillet; drain. Stir in taco seasoning, corn, tomatoes and green chilies, bell peppers and *1⅓ cups* French Fried Onions. Pour mixture into 2-quart oblong baking dish.

Prepare corn muffin mix according to package directions. Spoon batter around edge of beef mixture. Bake, uncovered, 20 minutes or until corn bread is golden. Top corn bread with cheese and remaining *1⅓ cups* onions. Bake, uncovered, 1 minute or until onions are golden.

Makes 6 servings

Prep Time: 15 minutes
Cook Time: 26 minutes

Chicken Bourguignonne

▮ ▮ ▮

4 pounds skinless chicken thighs and breasts
Flour
2 cups defatted low-sodium chicken broth
2 cups dry white wine or defatted low-sodium chicken broth
1 pound whole baby carrots
¼ cup tomato paste
4 cloves garlic, minced
½ teaspoon dried thyme leaves
2 bay leaves
¼ teaspoon salt
¼ teaspoon pepper
8 ounces fresh or thawed frozen pearl onions
8 ounces whole medium mushrooms
2 cups hot cooked white rice
2 cups hot cooked wild rice
¼ cup minced fresh parsley

Preheat oven to 325°F. Coat chicken very lightly with flour. Generously spray nonstick ovenproof Dutch oven or large nonstick ovenproof skillet with cooking spray; heat over medium heat until hot. Cook chicken 10 to 15 minutes or until browned on all sides. Drain fat from Dutch oven.

Add chicken broth, wine, carrots, tomato paste, garlic, thyme, bay leaves, salt and pepper to Dutch oven; heat to a boil. Cover; transfer to oven. Bake 1 hour. Add onions and mushrooms. Uncover; bake about 35 minutes or until vegetables are tender, and chicken is no longer pink in center and juices run clear. Remove bay leaves. Combine white and wild rice; serve with chicken. Sprinkle with parsley.

Makes 8 servings

Pork Chops and Yams

▮ ▮ ▮

4 pork chops (½-inch thick)
2 tablespoons oil
2 (16-ounce) cans yams, drained
½ large green bell pepper, cut into strips
2 tablespoons minced onion
¾ cup SMUCKER'S® Sweet Orange Marmalade or Apricot Preserves

Brown pork chops in oil over medium heat.

Place yams in 1½-quart casserole. Stir in green pepper, onions and marmalade. Layer pork chops over yam mixture. Cover and bake at 350° for 30 minutes or until pork chops are tender. *Makes 4 servings*

Contadina® Classic Lasagne

▌▌▌

1 tablespoon olive or
  vegetable oil
1 cup chopped onion
½ cup chopped green bell
  pepper
2 cloves garlic, minced
1½ pounds lean ground beef
2 cans (14.5 ounces each)
  CONTADINA® Diced
  Tomatoes, undrained
1 can (8 ounces)
  CONTADINA® Tomato
  Sauce
1 can (6 ounces)
  CONTADINA® Tomato
  Paste
½ cup dry red wine or beef
  broth
1½ teaspoons salt
1 teaspoon dried oregano
  leaves, crushed
1 teaspoon dried basil leaves,
  crushed
½ teaspoon ground black
  pepper
1 egg
1 cup (8 ounces) ricotta
  cheese
2 cups (8 ounces) shredded
  mozzarella cheese,
  divided
1 pound dry lasagne noodles,
  cooked, drained, kept
  warm

1. Heat oil in large skillet. Add onion, bell pepper and garlic; sauté for 3 minutes or until vegetables are tender.

2. Add beef; cook for 5 to 6 minutes or until evenly browned.

3. Add tomatoes and juice, tomato sauce, tomato paste, wine, salt, oregano, basil and black pepper; bring to a boil. Reduce heat to low; simmer, uncovered, for 20 minutes, stirring occasionally.

4. Beat egg slightly in medium bowl. Stir in ricotta cheese and 1 cup mozzarella cheese.

5. Layer noodles, half of meat sauce, noodles, all of ricotta cheese mixture, noodles and remaining meat sauce in ungreased 13×9-inch baking dish. Sprinkle with remaining mozzarella cheese.

6. Bake in preheated 350°F oven for 25 to 30 minutes or until heated through. Let stand for 10 minutes before cutting to serve.   *Makes 10 servings*

Prep Time: 35 minutes
Cook Time: 30 minutes
Standing Time: 10 minutes

Contadina® Classic Lasagne

Smoked Sausage and Sauerkraut Casserole

▮ ▮ ▮

6 fully-cooked smoked sausage links, such as German or Polish sausage (about 1½ pounds)
¼ cup packed brown sugar
2 tablespoons country-style Dijon mustard, Dijon mustard or German-style mustard
1 teaspoon caraway seed
½ teaspoon dill weed
1 jar (32 ounces) sauerkraut, drained
1 small green bell pepper, stemmed, seeded, diced
½ cup (2 ounces) shredded Swiss cheese

1. Place sausage in large skillet with ⅓ cup water. Cover; bring to a boil over medium heat. Reduce heat to low; simmer, covered, 10 minutes. Uncover and simmer until water evaporates and sausages brown lightly.

2. While sausage is cooking, combine sugar, mustard, caraway and dill in medium saucepan; stir until blended. Add sauerkraut and bell pepper; stir until well mixed. Cook, covered, over medium heat 10 minutes or until hot.

3. Spoon sauerkraut into microwavable 2- to 3-quart casserole; sprinkle with cheese.

Place sausage into sauerkraut; cover. Microwave on HIGH 30 seconds or until cheese melts.   *Makes 6 servings*

Prep and Cook Time: 20 minutes

Cook's Notes

Dijon mustard has a pale, grayish-yellow color and originally came from Dijon, France. Its flavor is clean and sharp and can range from mild to hot.

Smoked Sausage and Sauerkraut Casserole

Country Chicken Pot Pie

▌ ▌ ▌

2 tablespoons margarine or
butter
¾ pound boneless skinless
chicken breasts, cut into
1-inch pieces
¾ teaspoon salt
8 ounces fresh green beans,
cut into 1-inch pieces
(2 cups)
½ cup chopped red bell
pepper
½ cup thinly sliced celery
3 tablespoons all-purpose
flour
½ cup chicken broth
½ cup half-and-half
1 teaspoon dried thyme
leaves
½ teaspoon rubbed sage
1 cup frozen pearl onions
½ cup frozen corn
Pastry for single-crust
10-inch pie

Preheat oven to 425°F. Spray
10-inch deep-dish pie plate
with nonstick cooking spray.

Melt margarine in large deep
skillet over medium-high heat.
Add chicken; cook and stir
3 minutes or until no longer
pink in center. Sprinkle with
salt. Add beans, bell pepper
and celery; cook and stir
3 minutes.

Sprinkle flour evenly over
chicken and vegetables; cook
and stir 1 minute. Stir in broth,
half-and-half, thyme and sage;
bring to a boil over high heat.
Reduce heat to low and simmer
3 minutes or until sauce is very
thick. Stir in onions and corn.
Return to a simmer; cook and
stir 1 minute.

Transfer mixture to prepared
pie plate. Place pie crust over
chicken mixture; turn edge
under and crimp to seal. Cut
4 slits in pie crust to allow
steam to escape.

Bake 20 minutes or until crust
is light golden brown and
mixture is hot and bubbly. Let
stand 5 minutes before serving.
Makes 6 servings

Sausage and Cheese Potato Casserole

▌ ▌ ▌

1 pound BOB EVANS® Italian
Roll Sausage
4 cups cubed unpeeled red
skin potatoes
1 cup (4 ounces) shredded
Monterey Jack cheese
¼ cup chopped green onions
1 (4-ounce) can chopped
green chiles, drained
6 eggs
¾ cup milk
¼ teaspoon salt
⅛ teaspoon black pepper
½ cup grated Parmesan
cheese

Preheat oven to 350°F. Crumble and cook sausage in medium skillet until browned. Drain off any drippings. Spread potatoes in greased 13×9-inch baking pan. Top with cooked sausage, Monterey Jack cheese, green onions and chiles. Whisk eggs, milk, salt and pepper in medium bowl until frothy. Pour egg mixture over sausage layer; bake 30 minutes. Remove from oven. Sprinkle with Parmesan cheese; bake 15 minutes more or until eggs are set. Refrigerate leftovers.

Makes 6 to 8 servings

Ham & Macaroni Twists

▌▌▌

2 cups rotini or elbow macaroni, cooked in unsalted water and drained

1½ cups (8 ounces) cubed cooked ham

1⅓ cups FRENCH'S® French Fried Onions, divided

1 package (10 ounces) frozen broccoli spears, thawed and drained

1 cup milk

1 can (10¾ ounces) condensed cream of celery soup

1 cup (4 ounces) shredded Cheddar cheese, divided

¼ teaspoon garlic powder

¼ teaspoon pepper

Preheat oven to 350°F. In 12×8-inch baking dish, combine hot macaroni, ham and ⅔ *cup* French Fried Onions. Divide broccoli spears into 6 small bunches. Arrange bunches of spears down center of dish, alternating direction of flowerets. In small bowl, combine milk, soup, ½ cup cheese and the seasonings; pour over casserole. Bake, covered, at 350°F for 30 minutes or until heated through. Top with remaining cheese and sprinkle remaining ⅔ *cup* onions down center; bake, uncovered, 5 minutes or until onions are golden brown.

Makes 4 to 6 servings

Microwave Directions: In 12×8-inch microwave-safe dish, prepare macaroni mixture and arrange broccoli spears as above. Prepare soup mixture as above; pour over casserole. Cook, covered, on HIGH 8 minutes or until broccoli is done. Rotate dish halfway through cooking time. Top with remaining cheese and onions as above; cook, uncovered, 1 minute or until cheese melts. Let stand 5 minutes.

Savory Chicken and Biscuits

▌▌▌

1 pound boneless, skinless chicken thighs or breasts, cut into 1-inch pieces
1 medium potato, cut into 1-inch pieces
1 medium yellow onion, cut into 1-inch pieces
8 ounces fresh mushrooms, quartered
1 cup fresh baby carrots
1 cup chopped celery
1 (14½-ounce) can chicken broth
3 cloves garlic, minced
1 teaspoon dried rosemary leaves
1 teaspoon salt
1 teaspoon black pepper
3 tablespoons cornstarch blended with ½ cup cold water
1 cup frozen peas, thawed
1 (4-ounce) jar sliced pimentos, drained
1 package BOB EVANS® Frozen Buttermilk Biscuit Dough

Preheat oven to 375°F. Combine chicken, potato, onion, mushrooms, carrots, celery, broth, garlic, rosemary, salt and pepper in large saucepan. Bring to a boil over high heat. Reduce heat to low and simmer, uncovered, 5 minutes. Stir in cornstarch mixture; cook 2 minutes. Stir in peas and pimentos; return to a boil. Transfer chicken mixture to 2-quart casserole dish; arrange frozen biscuits on top. Bake 30 to 35 minutes or until biscuits are golden brown. Refrigerate leftovers.

Makes 4 to 6 servings

Serve It With Style!

To make this meal complete, just add a tossed green salad along with a slice of piping hot apple pie for dessert.

Savory Chicken and Biscuits

Tuna Noodle Casserole

▌▌▌

1 can (10¾ ounces) condensed cream of mushroom soup
1 cup milk
3 cups hot cooked rotini pasta (2 cups uncooked)
1 can (12.5 ounces) tuna packed in water, drained and flaked
1⅓ cups FRENCH'S® French Fried Onions, divided
1 package (10 ounces) frozen peas and carrots
½ cup (2 ounces) shredded Cheddar or grated Parmesan cheese

Combine soup and milk in 2-quart microwavable shallow casserole. Stir in pasta, tuna, ⅔ cup French Fried Onions, vegetables and cheese. Cover; microwave on HIGH 10 minutes* or until heated through, stirring halfway through cooking time. Top with remaining ⅔ cup onions. Microwave 1 minute or until onions are golden.

Makes 6 servings

Or, bake, covered, in 350°F oven 25 to 30 minutes.

Prep Time: 10 minutes
Cook Time: 11 minutes

Ham-Noodle Casserole

▌▌▌

1 can (10¾ ounces) condensed Cheddar cheese soup, undiluted
½ cup milk
½ cup sour cream
½ cup sliced celery
1 can (2½ ounces) sliced mushrooms, drained
2 cups diced HILLSHIRE FARM® Ham
3 ounces uncooked medium-size noodles, cooked and drained
¾ cup crushed rich round crackers
1 tablespoon butter or margarine, melted

Preheat oven to 375°F.

Combine soup, milk and sour cream in large bowl. Add celery and mushrooms. Stir in Ham and noodles. Pour mixture into medium casserole. Combine cracker crumbs and butter in small bowl; sprinkle over ham mixture. Bake, uncovered, 30 minutes or until hot and bubbly.   *Makes 6 servings*

Tuna Noodle Casserole

What's Your Beef?

Beef Pot Roast

▌▌▌

3 pounds beef eye of round
    roast
1 can (14 ounces) fat-free
    reduced-sodium beef
    broth
2 cloves garlic
1 teaspoon herbs de
    Provence *or* ¼ teaspoon
    each rosemary, thyme,
    sage and savory
4 small turnips, peeled and
    cut into wedges
10 ounces fresh brussels
    sprouts, trimmed
20 baby carrots
4 ounces pearl onions, outer
    skins removed
2 teaspoons cornstarch
    mixed with 1 tablespoon
    water

1. Heat large nonstick skillet over medium-high heat. Place roast, fat side down, in skillet. Cook until evenly browned. Remove roast from skillet; place in Dutch oven.

2. Pour broth into Dutch oven; bring to a boil over high heat. Add garlic and herbs de Provence. Cover tightly. Reduce heat; cook 1½ hours.

3. Add turnips, brussels sprouts, carrots and onions to Dutch oven. Cover; cook 25 to 30 minutes or until vegetables are tender. Remove meat and vegetables from Dutch oven. Arrange on serving platter; cover with foil to keep warm.

4. Strain broth; return to Dutch oven. Stir blended cornstarch mixture into broth. Bring to a boil over medium-high heat; cook and stir 1 minute or until thick and bubbly. Serve immediately with pot roast and vegetables. Garnish as desired.
Makes 6 servings

Beef Pot Roast

Swedish Meatballs

▌▌▌

1½ cups fresh bread crumbs
1 cup heavy cream
2 tablespoons butter or
    margarine, divided
1 small onion, chopped
1 pound ground beef
½ pound ground pork
3 tablespoons chopped fresh
    parsley, divided
1½ teaspoons salt
¼ teaspoon black pepper
¼ teaspoon ground allspice
1 cup beef broth
1 cup sour cream
1 tablespoon all-purpose flour

Combine bread crumbs and cream in small bowl; mix well. Let stand 10 minutes. Melt 1 tablespoon butter in large skillet over medium heat. Add onion. Cook and stir 5 minutes or until onion is tender. Combine beef, pork, bread crumb mixture, onion, 2 tablespoons parsley, salt, pepper and allspice in large bowl; mix well. Cover; refrigerate 1 hour.

Pat meat mixture into 1-inch-thick square on cutting board. Cut into 36 squares. Shape each square into a ball. Melt remaining 1 tablespoon butter in same large skillet over medium heat. Add meatballs. Cook 10 minutes or until browned on all sides and no longer pink in center. Remove meatballs from skillet; drain on paper towels.

Drain drippings from skillet; discard. Pour broth into skillet. Heat over medium-high heat, stirring frequently and scraping up any browned bits. Reduce heat to low.

Combine sour cream and flour; mix well. Stir sour cream mixture into skillet. Cook 5 minutes, stirring constantly. Do not boil. Add meatballs. Cook 5 minutes more. Sprinkle with remaining 1 tablespoon parsley. Garnish as desired.
Makes 5 to 6 servings

Note: Mashed potatoes, boiled red potatoes or broad egg noodles are wonderful accompaniments.

Swedish Meatballs

Hungarian Beef Rolls

▌▌▌

Spicy Tomato Sauce (recipe
  follows)
4 bacon slices, finely
  chopped
½ cup finely chopped onion
1 small clove garlic, minced
¾ pound lean ground beef
2 eggs, beaten
  Salt
  Dash freshly ground pepper
1 tablespoon paprika,
  Hungarian if possible
1½ pounds beef top round,
  sliced ½ inch thick
  (about 12 slices)
2 tablespoons vegetable oil

Prepare Spicy Tomato Sauce; keep warm while preparing beef rolls.

Cook bacon in medium skillet until partially cooked. Add onion and garlic; continue cooking until bacon is crisp and onion is tender. Drain.

Combine bacon mixture, ground beef, eggs and seasonings in medium bowl; mix lightly. Set aside.

Pound each beef slice to ¼-inch thickness. Spoon approximately 2 tablespoons ground beef mixture onto one end of each beef slice; roll to enclose filling. Secure with wooden pick or tie closed with kitchen string. Repeat with remaining beef slices and ground beef mixture.

Heat oil in large skillet. Add beef rolls in batches; cook until browned on all sides.

Add to Spicy Tomato Sauce; bring to a boil. Reduce heat; cover. Simmer 50 minutes or until beef is tender. Remove wooden picks before serving.

Makes 6 servings

SPICY TOMATO SAUCE
1 tablespoon vegetable oil
1 medium onion, chopped
1 clove garlic, minced
1 can (14½ ounces)
  tomatoes, crushed,
  undrained
2 cups chicken broth
2 tablespoons tomato paste
1 teaspoon paprika,
  Hungarian if possible
  Bay leaves
½ teaspoon salt
  Dash freshly ground pepper

Heat oil in large saucepan. Add onion and garlic; cook until tender. Stir in tomatoes with juice and remaining ingredients. Bring to a boil. Reduce heat; simmer until ready to use. Remove bay leaves just before serving.

Zesty Lemon-Glazed Steak

███

½ cup A.1.® Original or A.1.® BOLD & SPICY Steak Sauce
2 teaspoons grated lemon peel
1 clove garlic, minced
¼ teaspoon coarsely ground black pepper
¼ teaspoon dried oregano leaves
4 (4- to 6-ounce) beef shell steaks, about ½-inch thick

Blend steak sauce, lemon peel, garlic, pepper and oregano; brush on both sides of steaks. Grill steaks over medium heat or broil 6 inches from heat source 5 minutes on each side or to desired doneness, basting with sauce occasionally. Serve immediately.

Makes 4 servings

Zesty Onion Meatloaf

███

1½ pounds ground beef
1 can (10¾ ounces) condensed Italian tomato soup, divided
1⅓ cups FRENCH'S® French Fried Onions, divided
2 tablespoons FRENCH'S® Worcestershire Sauce
¾ teaspoon salt
¼ teaspoon ground pepper
1 egg

Preheat oven to 350°F. Combine beef, ⅓ cup soup, ⅔ *cup* French Fried Onions, Worcestershire, salt, pepper and egg in large bowl. Shape into 8×4-inch loaf. Place in shallow baking pan.

Bake 1 hour or until meat loaf is no longer pink in center and meat thermometer inserted in center registers 160°F. Pour off drippings; discard.

Spoon remaining soup over meatloaf. Top with remaining ⅔ *cup* onions. Bake 5 minutes or until onions are golden.

Makes 6 servings

Prep Time: 10 minutes
Cook Time: about 1 hour

Marinated Flank Steak with Pineapple

▌▌▌

1 can (15¼ ounces)
    DEL MONTE® Sliced
    Pineapple In Its Own
    Juice, undrained
¼ cup teriyaki sauce
2 tablespoons honey
1 pound flank steak

1. Drain pineapple, reserving 2 tablespoons juice. Set aside pineapple for later use.

2. Combine reserved juice, teriyaki sauce and honey in shallow 2-quart dish; mix well. Add meat; turn to coat. Cover and refrigerate at least 30 minutes or overnight.

3. Remove meat from marinade, reserving marinade. Grill meat over hot coals (or broil), brushing occasionally with reserved marinade. Cook about 4 minutes on each side for rare; about 5 minutes on each side for medium; or about 6 minutes on each side for well done. During last 4 minutes of cooking, brush pineapple slices with marinade; grill until heated through.

4. Slice meat across grain; serve with pineapple. Garnish, if desired.   *Makes 4 servings*

Note: Marinade that has come into contact with raw meat must be discarded or boiled for several minutes before serving with cooked food.

Prep and Marinate Time:
35 minutes
Cook Time: 10 minutes

Cook's Notes

Flank steak, a long, thin and boneless cut of beef, is a less expensive cut of meat. It is excellent when marinated, then grilled or broiled whole.

Marinated Flank Steak with Pineapple

Stuffed Salisbury Steak with Mushroom & Onion Topping

■ ■ ■

2 pounds ground beef
¼ cup FRENCH'S®
    Worcestershire Sauce
2⅔ cups FRENCH'S® French
    Fried Onions, divided
1 teaspoon garlic salt
½ teaspoon ground black
    pepper
4 ounces Cheddar cheese,
    cut into 6 sticks (about
    2×½×½ inches)
    Mushroom Topping (recipe
    follows)

Combine beef, Worcestershire, *1⅓ cups* French Fried Onions, garlic salt and pepper. Divide meat evenly into 6 portions. Place 1 stick cheese in center of each portion, firmly pressing and shaping meat into ovals around cheese.

Place steaks on grid. Grill over medium-high coals 15 minutes or until meat thermometer inserted into beef reaches 160°F, turning once. Serve with Mushroom Topping and sprinkle with remaining *1⅓ cups* onions.

Makes 6 servings

MUSHROOM TOPPING

2 tablespoons butter or
    margarine
1 package (12 ounces)
    mushrooms, wiped clean
    and quartered
2 tablespoons FRENCH'S®
    Worcestershire Sauce

Melt butter in large skillet over medium-high heat. Add mushrooms; cook 5 minutes or until browned, stirring often. Add Worcestershire. Reduce heat to low. Cook 5 minutes, stirring occasionally.

Makes 6 servings

Prep Time: 25 minutes
Cook Time: 25 minutes

Beef Stroganoff and Zucchini Topped Potatoes

■ ■ ■

4 baking potatoes (8 ounces
    each)
¾ pound ground beef round
¾ cup chopped onion
1 cup sliced mushrooms
1 beef bouillon cube
2 tablespoons ketchup
1 teaspoon Worcestershire
    sauce
¼ teaspoon freshly ground
    black pepper
¼ teaspoon hot pepper sauce
1 medium zucchini, cut into
    julienned strips
½ cup low-fat sour cream,
    divided

1. Pierce potatoes in several places with fork. Place in microwave oven on paper towel. Microwave potatoes at HIGH 15 minutes or until softened. Wrap in paper towels. Let stand 5 minutes.

2. Heat large nonstick skillet over medium-high heat until hot. Add beef and onion. Cook and stir 5 minutes or until beef is browned. Add all remaining ingredients except zucchini and sour cream. Cover and simmer 5 minutes. Add zucchini. Cover and cook 3 minutes. Remove from heat. Stir in ¼ cup sour cream. Cover and let stand 5 minutes.

3. Cut potatoes open. Divide beef mixture evenly among potatoes. Top with remaining ¼ cup sour cream.

Makes 4 servings

Prep and Cook Time: 25 minutes

Beef Stroganoff and Zucchini Topped Potato

LET THEM EAT CAKE

Scrumptious Apple Cake

▐ ▐ ▐

3 egg whites
1½ cups sugar
1 cup unsweetened
    applesauce
1 teaspoon vanilla
2 cups all-purpose flour
2 teaspoons ground
    cinnamon
1 teaspoon baking soda
¼ teaspoon salt
4 cups cored peeled tart
    apple slices (McIntosh or
    Crispin)
Yogurt Glaze (recipe
    follows)

Preheat oven to 350°F. Beat egg whites until slightly foamy; add sugar, applesauce and vanilla. Combine flour, cinnamon, baking soda and salt in separate bowl; add to applesauce mixture. Spread apples in 13×9-inch pan or 9-inch round springform pan sprayed with nonstick cooking spray. Spread batter over apples. Bake 35 to 40 minutes or until wooden toothpick inserted in center comes out clean; cool on wire rack. Prepare Yogurt Glaze; spread over cooled cake.

Makes 15 to 20 servings

Yogurt Glaze: Combine 1½ cups plain or vanilla nonfat yogurt, 3 tablespoons brown sugar (or to taste) and 1 teaspoon vanilla or 1 teaspoon lemon juice. Stir together until smooth.

Favorite recipe from **New York Apple Association**

Scrumptious Apple Cake

Hot Fudge Pudding Cake

Hot Fudge Pudding Cake

■■■

1¼ cups granulated sugar,
     divided
1 cup all-purpose flour
7 tablespoons HERSHEY'S
     Cocoa, divided
2 teaspoons baking powder
¼ teaspoon salt
½ cup milk
⅓ cup butter or margarine,
     melted
1½ teaspoons vanilla extract
½ cup packed light brown
     sugar
1¼ cups hot water
     Whipped topping

1. Heat oven to 350°F. Stir together ¾ cup granulated sugar, flour, 3 tablespoons cocoa, baking powder and salt. Stir in milk, butter and vanilla; beat until smooth.

2. Pour batter into ungreased 9-inch square baking pan. Stir together remaining ½ cup granulated sugar, brown sugar and remaining 4 tablespoons cocoa; sprinkle mixture evenly over batter. Pour hot water over top. Do not stir.

3. Bake 35 to 40 minutes or until center is almost set. Let stand 15 minutes; spoon into dessert dishes, spooning sauce from bottom of pan over top. Garnish with whipped topping.
     Makes about 8 servings

Prep Time: 10 minutes
Bake Time: 35 minutes
Cool Time: 15 minutes

Lemon Poppy Seed Cake

■ ■ ■

6 tablespoons margarine,
   softened
½ cup firmly packed light
   brown sugar
½ cup plain low fat yogurt
1 whole egg
2 egg whites
3 teaspoons fresh lemon
   juice
1¾ cups all-purpose flour
1 teaspoon baking powder
½ teaspoon baking soda
¼ teaspoon salt
⅓ cup fat-free (skim) milk
2 tablespoons poppy seeds
1 tablespoon grated lemon
   peel

LEMON GLAZE
1 cup powdered sugar
2½ tablespoons lemon juice
½ teaspoon poppy seed

1. Preheat oven to 350°F. Grease and flour 6-cup Bundt pan. Beat margarine in large bowl with electric mixer until fluffy. Beat in brown sugar, yogurt, whole egg, egg whites and 3 teaspoons lemon juice. Set aside.

2. Combine flour, baking powder, baking soda and salt in medium bowl. Add flour mixture to margarine mixture alternately with milk, beginning and ending with flour mixture. Mix in 2 tablespoons poppy seeds and lemon peel. Pour batter into prepared pan.

3. Bake about 40 minutes or until cake is golden brown and wooden pick inserted in center comes out clean. Cool in pan on wire rack 10 minutes; remove cake from pan and cool on wire rack.

4. For Lemon Glaze, mix powdered sugar with lemon juice until desired consistency. Spoon glaze over cake and sprinkle with ½ teaspoon poppy seed.

Makes 12 servings

New York Cheesecake

■■■

1 cup graham cracker crumbs
3 tablespoons sugar
3 tablespoons butter or
   margarine, melted
5 packages (8 ounces each)
   PHILADELPHIA® Cream
   Cheese, softened
1 cup sugar
3 tablespoons flour
1 tablespoon vanilla
3 eggs
1 cup BREAKSTONE'S® or
   KNUDSEN® Sour Cream

MIX crumbs, 3 tablespoons sugar and butter; press onto bottom of 9-inch springform pan. Bake at 350°F for 10 minutes.

MIX cream cheese, 1 cup sugar, flour and vanilla with electric mixer on medium speed until well blended. Add eggs, 1 at a time, mixing on low speed after each addition, just until blended. Blend in sour cream.

BAKE 1 hour and 5 minutes to 1 hour and 10 minutes or until center is almost set. Run knife or metal spatula around rim of pan to loosen cake; cool before removing rim of pan. Refrigerate 4 hours or overnight.

Makes 12 servings

Chocolate New York Cheesecake: Substitute 1 cup chocolate wafer cookie crumbs for graham cracker crumbs. Blend 8 squares BAKER'S® Semi-Sweet Chocolate, melted and slightly cooled, into batter. Continue as directed.

Lady Baltimore Cake

■■■

1¼ cups shortening
2¼ cups sugar
 2 teaspoons vanilla
3¼ cups all-purpose flour
4½ teaspoons baking powder
1½ teaspoons salt
1½ cups milk
 8 egg whites, at room
    temperature
   Filling (recipe page 69)
   Frosting (recipe page 69)

1. Preheat oven to 350°F. Grease three (9-inch) round cake pans.

2. Invert pan onto work surface. Place sheet of waxed paper over bottom of pan. Press around entire edge of pan to form crease in waxed paper. Cut along crease with scissors to form 9-inch circle. Repeat to make three circles. Place one circle in bottom of each pan.

3. Beat together shortening and sugar in large bowl until light and fluffy. Blend in vanilla.

4. Sift together dry ingredients. Add to sugar mixture

alternately with milk, beating well after each addition.

5. Beat egg whites in separate bowl at high speed with electric mixer until stiff peaks form; fold into batter. Pour evenly into prepared pans.

6. Bake 30 minutes or until wooden pick inserted in centers comes out clean. Cool layers in pans on wire racks 10 minutes. Loosen edges and remove to racks to cool completely. Prepare Filling and Frosting.

7. To assemble, spread two cake layers with Filling; stack on cake plate. Top with remaining cake layer. Frost with Frosting.

Makes one 3-layer cake

FILLING
½ cup (1 stick) butter or
   margarine
1 cup sugar
½ cup water
⅓ cup bourbon or brandy*
10 egg yolks, slightly beaten
1 cup finely chopped raisins
¾ cup chopped pecans
½ cup drained chopped
   maraschino cherries
½ cup flaked coconut
¾ teaspoon vanilla

Bourbon may be omitted. Increase water to ¾ cup. Add 1 tablespoon rum extract with vanilla.

1. Melt butter in 2-quart saucepan. Stir in sugar, water and bourbon. Bring to a boil over medium-high heat, stirring occasionally to dissolve sugar.

2. Stir small amount of hot mixture into egg yolks. Add egg yolk mixture to remaining hot mixture in saucepan. Cook until thickened; remove from heat.

3. Stir in raisins, pecans, cherries and coconut. Blend in vanilla. Cool completely.

FROSTING
1½ cups sugar
½ cup water
2 egg whites**
2 teaspoons corn syrup or
   ¼ teaspoon cream of
   tartar
Dash of salt
1 teaspoon vanilla

Use clean, uncracked eggs.

1. Combine sugar, water, egg whites, corn syrup and salt in top of double boiler. Beat 30 seconds.

2. Place on top of range; cook, stirring occasionally, over simmering water 7 minutes.

3. Remove from heat; add vanilla. Beat 3 minutes or until frosting is of spreading consistency.

Banana-Nut Cake

▌▌▌

2½ cups all-purpose flour
1 teaspoon salt
¾ teaspoon baking powder
¾ teaspoon baking soda
⅔ cup shortening
1⅔ cups sugar
2 eggs
1¼ cups mashed ripe bananas
   (2 to 3 medium bananas)
⅔ cup buttermilk, divided
⅔ cup chopped walnuts
   Creamy Frosting (recipe
      follows)
   Banana slices and fresh
      mint leaves for garnish

1. Preheat oven to 375°F. Grease and flour two (9-inch) round cake pans.

2. Combine flour, salt, baking powder and baking soda in medium bowl; set aside.

3. Beat together shortening and sugar in large bowl until light and fluffy. Add eggs, one at a time, beating well after each addition. Blend in bananas.

4. Add flour mixture alternately with buttermilk, beating well after each addition. Stir in walnuts. Pour evenly into prepared pans.

5. Bake 30 to 35 minutes or until wooden pick inserted in centers comes out clean. Cool in pans on wire racks 10 minutes. Loosen edges; remove to racks to cool completely.

6. Fill and frost with Creamy Frosting. Run pastry comb across top and around side of cake, if desired, for ridged effect. Garnish, if desired.

Makes one 2-layer cake

CREAMY FROSTING

⅓ cup plus 2 tablespoons
   all-purpose flour
   Dash of salt
1 cup milk
½ cup shortening
½ cup (1 stick) margarine,
   softened
1¼ cups granulated sugar
1 teaspoon vanilla

1. Combine flour and salt in 2-quart saucepan. Gradually stir in milk until well blended. Cook over medium heat until thickened, stirring constantly. Cool.

2. Beat together shortening and margarine in large bowl until creamy. Add sugar; beat until light and fluffy. Blend in vanilla. Add cooled flour mixture; beat until smooth.

Banana-Nut Cake

Double Chocolate Bundt Cake

▮ ▮ ▮

1 package (about 18 ounces) chocolate cake mix
1 package (4-serving size) instant chocolate pudding mix
4 eggs, beaten
¾ cup water
¾ cup sour cream
½ cup oil
6 ounces (1 cup) semisweet chocolate chips
Powdered sugar

1. Preheat oven to 350°F. Spray 10-inch Bundt or tube pan with nonstick cooking spray.

2. Beat cake mix, pudding mix, eggs, water, sour cream and oil in large bowl with electric mixer at medium speed until ingredients are blended. Stir in chocolate chips; pour into prepared pan.

3. Bake 55 to 60 minutes or until cake springs back when lightly touched. Cool 1 hour in pan on wire rack. Invert cake onto serving plate; cool completely. Sprinkle with powdered sugar before serving.

Makes 10 to 12 servings

Spicy Gingerbread

▮ ▮ ▮

2 cups all-purpose flour
1 cup light molasses
¾ cup buttermilk
½ cup granulated sugar
½ cup FLEISCHMANN'S® Original Margarine, softened
¼ cup EGG BEATERS® Healthy Real Egg Substitute
2 teaspoons baking soda
1 teaspoon ground cinnamon
½ teaspoon ground ginger
¼ teaspoon ground cloves
Powdered sugar, optional

In large bowl, with electric mixer at low speed, beat flour, molasses, buttermilk, granulated sugar, margarine, Egg Beaters, baking soda, cinnamon, ginger and cloves until moistened; scrape down side and bottom of bowl. Beat at medium speed for 3 minutes. Spread batter into greased 9-inch square baking pan. Bake at 350°F for 1 hour or until toothpick inserted in center comes out clean. Cool in pan on wire rack. Dust with powdered sugar before serving if desired. Cut into 16 (2-inch) squares. *Makes 16 servings*

Prep Time: 20 minutes
Cook Time: 1 hour

Double Chocolate Bundt Cake

Pie in the Sky

Country Apple Rhubarb Pie

CRUST
9-inch Classic CRISCO®
Double Crust (page 82)

FILLING
9 cups sliced, peeled Granny
   Smith apples (about
   3 pounds or 6 large
   apples)
1½ cups chopped (about
   ½ inch) fresh rhubarb,
   peeled if tough
¾ cup granulated sugar
½ cup firmly packed light
   brown sugar
2 tablespoons all-purpose flour
1 tablespoon cornstarch
1 teaspoon ground cinnamon
¼ teaspoon freshly grated
   nutmeg

GLAZE
1 egg, beaten
1 tablespoon water
1 tablespoon granulated
   sugar
1 teaspoon ground pecans or
   walnuts
⅛ teaspoon ground cinnamon

1. For crust, prepare dough. Roll and press bottom crust into 9- or 9½-inch deep-dish pie plate. Heat oven to 425°F.

2. For filling, combine apples and rhubarb in large bowl. Combine ¾ cup granulated sugar, brown sugar, flour, cornstarch, 1 teaspoon cinnamon and nutmeg in medium bowl. Sprinkle over fruit; toss. Spoon into pie crust. Moisten pastry edge with water. Cover pie with lattice top, cutting strips 1 inch wide. Flute edge.

3. For glaze, combine egg and water in small bowl. Brush over crust. Combine remaining glaze ingredients in small bowl. Sprinkle over crust.

4. Bake at 425°F for 20 minutes. *Reduce oven temperature to 350°F.* Bake 30 to 40 minutes or until filling in center is bubbly and crust is golden brown. Place sheet of foil under pie if it starts to bubble over. Cool.
   Makes 1 pie (8 servings)

Country Apple Rhubarb Pie

Crunch Peach Cobbler

▌▐▌▐▌

1 can (29 ounces) *or* 2 cans
      (16 ounces each) cling
      peach slices in syrup
⅓ cup plus 1 tablespoon
      granulated sugar, divided
1 tablespoon cornstarch
½ teaspoon vanilla
2 cups all-purpose flour,
      divided
½ cup packed brown sugar
⅓ cup uncooked old-fashioned
      or quick oats
¼ cup margarine or butter,
      melted
½ teaspoon ground cinnamon
½ teaspoon salt
½ cup shortening
4 to 5 tablespoons cold
      water
Whipped cream for garnish

1. Drain peach slices in fine-meshed sieve over 2-cup glass measure. Reserve ¾ cup syrup.

2. Combine ⅓ cup granulated sugar and cornstarch in small saucepan. Slowly add reserved syrup. Stir well. Add vanilla. Cook over low heat, stirring constantly, until thickened. Set aside.

3. Combine ½ cup flour, brown sugar, oats, margarine and cinnamon in small bowl; stir until mixture forms coarse crumbs. Set aside.

4. Preheat oven to 350°F. Combine remaining 1½ cups flour, 1 tablespoon granulated sugar and salt in small bowl. Cut in shortening with pastry blender or 2 knives until mixture forms pea-sized pieces. Sprinkle water, 1 tablespoon at a time, over flour mixture. Toss lightly with fork until mixture holds together. Press together to form a ball.

5. Roll out dough into 10-inch square, ⅛ inch thick. Fold dough in half, then in half again. Carefully place folded dough in center of 8 × 8-inch baking dish. Unfold and press onto bottom and about 1 inch up sides of dish. Arrange peaches over crust. Pour sauce over peaches. Sprinkle with crumb topping.

6. Bake 45 minutes. Serve warm or at room temperature with whipped cream.
      Makes about 6 servings

Crunch Peach Cobbler

COOKING CLASS

Cut the shortening into flour with pastry blender.

Toss shortening mixture and water lightly with fork until dough forms a ball.

Press dough between hands to form 5- to 6-inch "pancake."

Classic Crisco®
Double Crust

■ ■ ■

2 cups all-purpose flour
1 teaspoon salt
¾ CRISCO® Stick or ¾ cup Crisco
   all-vegetable shortening
5 tablespoons cold water (or more as
   needed)

1. Combine flour and salt in medium bowl.

2. Cut in shortening using pastry blender (or 2 knives) until all flour is blended in to form pea-size chunks (see photo).

3. Sprinkle with water, 1 tablespoon at a time. Toss lightly with fork until dough forms a ball (see photo).

4. Divide dough in half. Press between hands to form two 5- to 6-inch "pancakes" (see photo).

5. Traditional rolling technique: Flour dough lightly. Roll dough for bottom crust into circle between sheets of waxed paper on dampened countertop. Peel off top sheet. Trim 1 inch larger than inverted 9-inch pie plate. Loosen dough carefully. Fold into quarters. Unfold and press into pie plate.

6. Easy rolling technique: Flour dough lightly. Roll dough for bottom crust into circle between sheets of waxed paper on dampened countertop. Peel off top sheet. Trim one inch larger than inverted 9-inch pie plate. Slip into pie plate (see photo). Remove other sheet and press pastry to fit.

7. To assemble, trim edge of bottom crust even with edge of pie plate. Add filling to unbaked pie shell. Moisten pastry edge with water. Roll top crust same as bottom. Lift top crust onto filled pie (see photo). Trim ½ inch beyond edge of pie plate. Fold top edge under bottom crust. Flute. Cut slits in top crust or prick with fork for escape of steam. Bake according to filling recipes.

Makes 1 (9-inch) double crust

Slip bottom crust into pie plate.

Lift top crust onto filled pie.

New York Apple Maple Cream Pie (page 92)

Cranberry Apple Nut Pie

■ ■ ■

Rich Pie Pastry (recipe follows)
1 cup sugar
3 tablespoons all-purpose flour
¼ teaspoon salt
4 cups sliced peeled tart apples (4 large apples)
2 cups fresh cranberries
½ cup golden raisins
½ cup coarsely chopped pecans
1 tablespoon grated lemon peel
2 tablespoons butter or margarine
1 egg, beaten

Preheat oven to 425°F. Divide pie pastry in half. Roll one half on lightly floured surface to form 13-inch circle. Fit into 9-inch pie plate; trim edges. Reroll scraps and cut into decorative shapes, such as holly leaves and berries, for garnish; set aside.

Combine sugar, flour and salt in large bowl. Stir in apples, cranberries, raisins, pecans and lemon peel; toss well. Spoon fruit mixture into unbaked pie crust. Dot with butter. Roll remaining half of pie pastry on lightly floured surface to form 11-inch circle. Place over filling. Trim and seal edges; flute. Cut 3 slits in center of top crust. Moisten pastry cutouts and decorate as desired. Lightly brush top crust with egg.

Bake 35 to 40 minutes or until apples are tender when pierced with a fork and pastry is golden brown. Cool in pan on wire rack. Serve warm or cool completely.

Makes 1 (9-inch) pie

RICH PIE PASTRY
2 cups all-purpose flour
¼ teaspoon salt
6 tablespoons butter
6 tablespoons lard
6 to 8 tablespoons cold water

Combine flour and salt in medium bowl. Cut in butter and lard with pastry blender or 2 knives until mixture resembles coarse crumbs. Sprinkle water, 1 tablespoon at a time, over flour mixture, mixing until flour is moistened. Shape dough into a ball. Roll, fill and bake as recipe directs.

Makes pastry for 1 (9-inch) double pie crust

Note: For single crust, cut recipe in half.

Cranberry Apple Nut Pie

Fresh Fruit Tart

▌▌▌

1⅔ cups all-purpose flour
⅓ cup sugar
¼ teaspoon salt
½ cup butter or margarine,
    softened and cut into
    pieces
1 egg yolk
2 to 3 tablespoons milk
1 package (8 ounces) regular
    or reduced-calorie cream
    cheese, softened
⅓ cup strawberry jam
2 to 3 cups mixed assorted
    fresh fruit, such as sliced
    bananas, sliced kiwi,
    blueberries, sliced
    peaches, sliced plums,
    raspberries and halved
    strawberries
¼ cup apple jelly, melted
¼ cup toasted sliced
    unblanched almonds
    (optional)

1. Combine flour, sugar and salt in food processor or blender; process until just combined. Add butter. Process using on/off pulsing action until mixture resembles coarse crumbs. Add egg yolk and 2 tablespoons milk; process until dough leaves side of bowl. Add additional milk by teaspoons, if necessary. Shape dough into a disc. Wrap in plastic wrap and refrigerate 30 minutes or until firm.

2. Preheat oven to 350°F. Roll dough out on lightly floured surface to ¼-inch thickness. Cut 12-inch circle; transfer to 10-inch tart pan with removable bottom. Press lightly onto bottom and up side of pan; trim edge even with edge of pan. Bake 16 to 18 minutes or until light golden brown. Transfer to wire rack; cool completely.

3. Combine cream cheese and jam in small bowl; mix well. Spread evenly over cooled crust. Arrange fruit decoratively over cream cheese layer. Brush fruit with apple jelly. Sprinkle with almonds, if desired. Serve immediately or refrigerate up to 2 hours before serving.

Makes 8 servings

Fresh Fruit Tart

CLASSY CRUSTS

You too can create decorative pie crusts like a pro. Simply choose one of the techniques below to create a pie crust that looks like it just came out of a bakery.

Pinwheel

Fold overhang of bottom crust under; press flat. Cut slits around edge of pastry the width of the pie plate rim, leaving about 1 inch between slits. Fold under on a diagonal to form pinwheel points.

Rope Edge

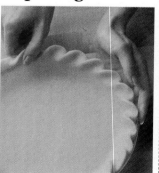

Fold overhang of bottom crust under and make stand-up edge. Press thumb into pastry at an angle. Pinch pastry between thumb and knuckle of index finger, rolling knuckle towards thumb. Place thumb in groove left by finger and continue around edge.

Fork Edge

Trim edge of bottom crust even with pie plate. Press to rim of pie plate using 4-tined fork. Leave about 1¼ inches between marks. Go around crust edge again, filling in spaces with fork held at an angle.

Cut Outs

Trim edge of bottom crust even with pie plate. Cut desired shapes from remaining pastry using tiny cookie cutter, thimble or bottlecap. Moisten pastry edge. Place cutouts on pastry edge, slightly overlapping. Press into place.

Woven Lattice Top

Leave overhang on bottom crust. Cut top crust into ten ½-inch strips. Place 5 strips evenly across filling. Fold every other strip back. Lay first strip across in opposite direction. Continue in this pattern, folding back every other strip each time you add a cross strip. Trim ends of lattice strips even with crust overhang; press together. Fold edge under; flute.

Black Raspberry Pie

■ ■ ■

CRUST
  Classic CRISCO® Double Crust (recipe page 82)

FILLING
  4 cups fresh or frozen black raspberries
1¼ cups sugar
  ¼ cup cornstarch
  2 tablespoons butter or margarine, softened
  Dash salt

1. For crust, prepare as directed. Roll and press bottom crust into 9-inch pie plate. Do not bake. Heat oven to 350°F.

2. For filling, combine raspberries, sugar, cornstarch, butter and salt. Toss gently. Spoon into unbaked pie crust. Moisten pastry edge with water.

3. Roll top crust same as bottom. Lift onto filled pie. Trim ½ inch beyond edge of pie plate. Fold top edge under bottom crust. Flute. Cut slits in top crust to allow steam to escape.

4. Bake at 350°F for 1 hour or until filling in center is bubbly and crust is golden brown. *Do not overbake.* Cool to room temperature before serving.
  Makes 1 (9-inch) pie

Tip: Try red raspberries if black raspberries are unavailable.

Cook's Notes

If using frozen black raspberries, partially thaw them before preparing filling.

Libby's® Famous Pumpkin Pie

■ ■ ■

¾ cup granulated sugar
½ teaspoon salt
1 teaspoon ground cinnamon
½ teaspoon ground ginger
¼ teaspoon ground cloves
2 eggs
**1 can (15-ounce) LIBBY'S®
    100% Pure Pumpkin**
**1 can (12 fluid-ounce)
    NESTLÉ® CARNATION®
    Evaporated Milk***
**1 *unbaked* 9-inch (4-cup
    volume) deep-dish pie
    shell**
Whipped cream

*For lower fat/calorie pie, substitute
CARNATION® Evaporated Lowfat Milk
or Evaporated Fat Free Milk.*

MIX sugar, salt, cinnamon,
ginger and cloves in small
bowl. Beat eggs in large bowl.
Stir in pumpkin, and sugar-
spice mixture. Gradually stir in
evaporated milk.

POUR into pie shell.

BAKE in preheated 425°F. oven
for 15 minutes. Reduce
temperature to 350°F.; bake
40 to 50 minutes or until knife
inserted near center comes out
clean. Cool on wire rack for
2 hours. Serve immediately or
refrigerate. Top with whipped
cream before serving.

FOR 2 SHALLOW PIES,
substitute two 9-inch (2-cup
volume) pie shells. Bake in
preheated 425°F. oven for
15 minutes. Reduce temperature
to 350°F.; bake for 20 to
30 minutes or until pies test
done.   *Makes 8 servings*

To add a splash of splendor to this
traditional pie, pipe whipped cream
around the edge in a decorative
pattern.

Libby's® Famous Pumpkin Pie

New York Apple Maple Cream Pie

■ ■ ■

CRUST
   1 unbaked 9-inch Classic
      CRISCO® Double Crust
      (page 82)

FILLING
   6 cups sliced, peeled baking
      apples* (about 2 pounds
      or 6 medium)
   1 cup sugar
   3 tablespoons cornstarch
   ½ teaspoon salt
   ¾ cup pure maple syrup**
   ½ cup whipping cream

GLAZE
      Milk
      Sugar

Golden Delicious, Granny Smith and Jonathan apples are suitable for pie baking.

**Substitute maple-flavored pancake and waffle syrup, if desired.*

1. Heat oven to 400°F.

2. For crust, prepare dough. Roll and press bottom crust into 9-inch pie plate. Do not bake. Reserve dough scraps for decoration, if desired; roll out and cut into desired shapes using cookie cutter. Arrange on baking sheet; set aside.

3. For filling, place apples, 1 cup sugar, cornstarch and salt in large bowl. Toss to coat. Combine maple syrup and whipping cream in small bowl. Pour over apple mixture. Mix gently. Spoon into unbaked pie crust. Moisten pastry edge with water.

4. Roll out top crust. Lift onto filled pie. Trim ½ inch beyond edge of pie plate. Fold top edge under bottom crust; flute. Decorate with pastry cutouts, if desired. Cut slits into top crust to allow steam to escape.

5. For glaze, brush crust with milk. Sprinkle with sugar.

6. Bake at 400°F for 50 to 60 minutes or until filling in center is bubbly and crust is golden brown. Refrigerate leftover pie.

Makes 1 (9-inch) pie

The publisher would like to thank the companies and organizations listed below for the use of their recipes and photographs in this publication.

A.1.® Steak Sauce

Bob Evans®

Colorado Potato Administrative Committee

ConAgra Foods®

Del Monte Corporation

Dole Food Company, Inc.

Egg Beaters®

Grey Poupon® Dijon Mustard

Hershey Foods Corporation

The Hidden Valley® Food Products Company

Hillshire Farm®

Kraft Foods Holdings

McIlhenny Company (TABASCO® brand Pepper Sauce)

Nestlé USA

New York Apple Association, Inc.

Reckitt Benckiser

RED STAR® Yeast, a product of Lasaffre Yeast Corporation

Roman Meal® Company

The J.M. Smucker Company

Walnut Marketing Board

Washington Apple Commission

METRIC CONVERSION CHART

VOLUME MEASUREMENTS (dry)

$1/8$ teaspoon = 0.5 mL
$1/4$ teaspoon = 1 mL
$1/2$ teaspoon = 2 mL
$3/4$ teaspoon = 4 mL
1 teaspoon = 5 mL
1 tablespoon = 15 mL
2 tablespoons = 30 mL
$1/4$ cup = 60 mL
$1/3$ cup = 75 mL
$1/2$ cup = 125 mL
$2/3$ cup = 150 mL
$3/4$ cup = 175 mL
1 cup = 250 mL
2 cups = 1 pint = 500 mL
3 cups = 750 mL
4 cups = 1 quart = 1 L

VOLUME MEASUREMENTS (fluid)

1 fluid ounce (2 tablespoons) = 30 mL
4 fluid ounces ($1/2$ cup) = 125 mL
8 fluid ounces (1 cup) = 250 mL
12 fluid ounces ($1 1/2$ cups) = 375 mL
16 fluid ounces (2 cups) = 500 mL

WEIGHTS (mass)

$1/2$ ounce = 15 g
1 ounce = 30 g
3 ounces = 90 g
4 ounces = 120 g
8 ounces = 225 g
10 ounces = 285 g
12 ounces = 360 g
16 ounces = 1 pound = 450 g

DIMENSIONS

$1/16$ inch = 2 mm
$1/8$ inch = 3 mm
$1/4$ inch = 6 mm
$1/2$ inch = 1.5 cm
$3/4$ inch = 2 cm
1 inch = 2.5 cm

OVEN TEMPERATURES

250°F = 120°C
275°F = 140°C
300°F = 150°C
325°F = 160°C
350°F = 180°C
375°F = 190°C
400°F = 200°C
425°F = 220°C
450°F = 230°C

BAKING PAN SIZES

Utensil	Size in Inches/Quarts	Metric Volume	Size in Centimeters
Baking or Cake Pan (square or rectangular)	$8 \times 8 \times 2$	2 L	$20 \times 20 \times 5$
	$9 \times 9 \times 2$	2.5 L	$23 \times 23 \times 5$
	$12 \times 8 \times 2$	3 L	$30 \times 20 \times 5$
	$13 \times 9 \times 2$	3.5 L	$33 \times 23 \times 5$
Loaf Pan	$8 \times 4 \times 3$	1.5 L	$20 \times 10 \times 7$
	$9 \times 5 \times 3$	2 L	$23 \times 13 \times 7$
Round Layer Cake Pan	$8 \times 1 1/2$	1.2 L	20×4
	$9 \times 1 1/2$	1.5 L	23×4
Pie Plate	$8 \times 1 1/4$	750 mL	20×3
	$9 \times 1 1/4$	1 L	23×3
Baking Dish or Casserole	1 quart	1 L	—
	$1 1/2$ quart	1.5 L	—
	2 quart	2 L	—